An Introduction to Angels & Angelic Healing

Learn to connect to your Angels & start your Angelic Healing today...

Jodi Cross

BALBOA.
PRESS
A DIVISION OF HAY HOUSE

ISBN: 978-1-4525-5649-9 (sc)
ISBN: 978-1-4525-5650-5 (e)

Balboa Press books may be ordered through booksellers or by contacting:

Balboa Press
A Division of Hay House
1663 Liberty Drive
Bloomington, IN 47403
www.balboapress.com
1-(877) 407-4847

Printed in the United States of America

Balboa Press rev. date: 8/24/2012

I dedicate this book to the

Love and Light of God &

his beloved Angels,

To my loving parents,

Edna & Ken Leatherland,

my

wonderful husband

Peter

&

My gifted children

Emma,

Mark & Luke.

Bless you all for your love, help & support.

Introduction.
About the Author...

Rev. Jodi Cross, 'The Angel Minister', grew up in a beautiful little Northamptonshire village called Hollowell. With houses nestling on the side of a pretty green valley complete with a crystal clear babbling brook meandering its way through the little village.

Hollowell can be traced back to the Doomsday Book and was logged as a small hamlet of Guilsborough known as

'Holy Well.'

The village church, St James, has a very special place in her heart.

'The church has a lovely energy and is where I first met and got to know my spiritual family. The very first time I was taken into St James an incredible feeling of peace came over me and it still has the same effect today. As a very young child I can remember listening to bible stories at Sunday School and learning about the life of Jesus.'

'I was thrilled to learn that God chose Joseph the Carpenter to be Jesus' daddy. Wow!

I remember feeling very honoured that Jesus and I had something in common, as my own father was also a Carpenter!

Like most little girls, I placed my father high on a pedestal, he was my very own super hero and, in fact, he still is! '

'St James was a very important part of my life as a child. My granny took me to church every Sunday just as soon as I was able to read and therefore follow the service'

' I was taught that the church was a very special place that had to be respected because this was the place that you could speak directly to God, through prayer. Ladies always wore hats and their Sunday best suits and the men would have their smartest outfit combed greased hair and shiny shoes. My granny had her own prayer book which was always carried in her gloved hands with the respect and reverence that you would give a Holy Relic.

I was soon asked to join the choir and remained a member of that family for many happy years. There were only four of us in the choir, it was such a small village in those days, but we did our best. I always felt as if it was my second home. I felt at peace there, totally connected. And when my soul has finished with this human body and I ascend to be with my spiritual family, I shall be buried there with my ancestors and family.'

Jodi has been working with the Angels, Lord Jesus and other Ascended Masters for many years and has a regular Reflexology and Reiki Clinic as well as running Angel Therapy Clinics, Workshops, Courses, and Angel Ministry Services to help people find peace, health and happiness, and to find a deeper connection to the light.

Jodi is an Interfaith Angel Minister of the Order of the Seraphim, also an Advanced Angel Therapy Practitioner®, a

Holistic Therapist, a Reiki Master Teacher, a Magnified Healing Practitioner, a Member of the International Council of Holistic Therapists and a student of 'A Course in Miracles'.

Over the past few years Jodi has channelled numerous prayers, services, affirmations and the beginnings of two other books still in progress.

Famous deceased artists such as John Lennon and Heath Ledger have also channelled messages to Jodi.

Included in this book are prints of some of the paintings and drawings that the Angels have channelled to Jodi. Each one has a unique message and energy.

Jodi now lives in Buckinghamshire, England with her beloved husband Peter and her two youngest children. The family share their home with two rescue cats, Charlie and Magic.

When time allows, Jodi and her family enjoy spending time in France relaxing and exploring the medieval towns and villages along the Dordogne valley.

©Angelic Essence of Cherubim. Copyright Rev. Jodi Cross 2012

' This book has been channelled for you, the reader, to learn how to connect with your own Angelic guides and Angelic Healing but also to understand the importance, and the ability, that each one of us has in bringing more love, light and healing to our own lives; to regain our inner peace and to bring harmony love, light and healing, to this planet we call home. '

'We are all one, we all live together in God's love upon this precious earth, this life of ours is a gift, don't waste it, use it wisely'

'Remember, each and every one of you have been created as a perfect child of God, the help and support that you have in Angelic guidance is unlimited as is their profound depth of unconditional love for you.'

©Child of the Light. Copyright Rev. Jodi Cross 2012

CHAPTER I

Who, What, Where are the Angels

The word Angel comes from the Greek word ANGELOS meaning MESSENGER. Angels are our personal communication channel, to and from, our creator. MESSENGERS sent to us by our creator to act as a bridge between our world and Source.

Everything on and within our planet is created from energy. Everything within our planets energy has its own vibrational frequency; Humans, Animals, Liquids, Gases, the Flora and Fauna, and the Rocks and Crystals that make up our planet, all have their own, individual, vibrational frequency.

The slower the frequency, the denser the matter. We humans vibrate at a lower frequency than the Angelic realm, therefore our three dimensional human senses are not necessarily the best tools to use to see, hear, feel or know when Angels are trying to connect to us.

We have come to know these beings of light, or Angels, as our very own link to the creator. We all have different names that we use for the 'Energy of Creation' depending where we were bought up, and to what particular religious belief system we belong to; but whether we use the word, or name, God, Source, Allah, Jehovah, Father Creator, Big Bang, God Most High In The Universe or a number of other names that we have come to know, we are all talking about the same energy, the same force, the same creator.

(I prefer to use the name Source, or God, when I am talking about our creator and have used these words throughout this book)

Angels are **non** denominational. This means that they are not associated to any one individual specific sect or religion. They are from and of God and are recognised across our planet in many of our different holy and revered scriptures.

You will of course find Angels in the Christian teachings, the Bible. In the Old Testament you will find seventeen references to the Angels appearances, and the use of the word Angel appears many more times throughout the Old Testament.

It was in the New Testament that the Angels spoke to Mary about her carrying the baby Jesus, they spoke to Joseph explaining to him that Marys child was sent from God, they spoke to the Shepherds on the hills, the Magi after seeing the King, and numerous other times and tales regarding Angels coming to help, warn or deliver messages, in fact the word Angel is used one hundred and sixty-five times in the New Testament.

However you will also find them in the Jewish teachings, the Torah, and also in the Muslim faith, the Qur'an.

It is believed that the Qur'an was channelled to the Prophet Mohamed, (Peace be upon him) by the Archangel Gabriel.

In fact in most of the large recognised religions of our world today, you will find some form or variation of Angels.

Here in the UK or Europe, if you are lucky enough to live in, or around, an old established town or city, you are likely to be surrounded by artistic interpretations of angels.

Angels are often depicted as a human form with wings.

It is understandable that visual interpretations have some form of wings as they are usually surrounded by energy that seems to emit light.

It is this light that radiates outward from within and the fact that they will often appear from above that gives a sense of wings.

©Angel of the Heart. Copyright Rev. J Cross 2012 .

As you wander around your local town or city you will probably find a number of statues of Angels, looking down at you from buildings, even in the middle of roundabouts and road interchanges. Not to mention the many hundreds that may adorn our religious buildings either in statue form or in the beautiful stained glass windows. In fact we are so use to them being around us that we often don't even notice that they are there.

Today as I write this I have been dipping in and out of the TV broadcasts celebrating Queen Elizabeth's Diamond Jubilee and have noticed members of the clergy greeting her majesty at the doors of St Pauls, with beautiful gold embroidered Angels on their backs. Later as the crowds walk up the Mall and look towards the palace for the Queens Balcony appearance, their gaze will be met by a beautiful Golden Angel standing above Queen Victoria's monument.

When wandering around shops and stores you will notice Angels depicted on mugs, cards, items of clothing, jewellery, mirrors, candlesticks and a variety of other household goods. Next time you visit your local metropolis have a good look around. You'll be surprised how many there are.

Artistic interpretations, both old and new, of Angels, are all around us as we go about our daily life. Libraries and the internet are, of course, a good source of information on the subject, as are the Holy Books already mentioned.

Dating back throughout our history, we have a wealth of information on the subject of Angels. And yet we still find them new and exciting. Perhaps that is because our personal relationship with our own Angels is a new and exciting one.

The reason that you have bought this book is to find out how you can enhance your own relationship with your very own Angels as well as to start the Angelic Healing process, healing different aspects of your life.

As we start to learn about the Angelic Realm, one of the first things to note is that literature suggests that there are Nine different orders of Angelic Energies. They are grouped into threes.

The first energetic order, nearest to our creator, with the highest vibrational frequency is

1. Seraphim

2. Cherubim

3. Thrones

The second energetic order is

4. Dominions

5. Virtues

6. Powers

And the third energetic order, the nearest orders to our world are

- Principalities

- Archangels

- Angels

The different orders all have slightly different functions. The highest vibrational group, Seraphim, Cherubim and Thrones are seen as being closest to God, whilst the lower vibrational frequency group, the Principalities, Archangels and Angels are seen as the closest to Earth and its inhabitants.

There are those who feel that rather than seeing the Order of The Angelic Realm as a line, from God to Earth, that it is more appropriate to see it as a 'sphere' of Angelic Energy working together in perfect harmony to create Gods Army of Light throughout the universes.

Archangels tend to be larger in stature than Angels.

Here are the names and some information about four of the better known Archangels that we can see depicted in our towns and cities and that we have perhaps read about in our scriptures.

*

Archangel Michael.

Michael is often depicted with his 'Sword of Truth'

He is recognised as the Archangel who Protects, with his Sword of Truth and his Shield of Strength, and is accepted as the patron of the Police force.

When Archangel Michaels energy is present he is associated with the colour blue.

Some see this as royal blue or purple blue, others as more of a petrol blue.

When I work with Michael the temperature changes and I can feel his warmth.

The meaning of his name is

WHO IS LIKE GOD

*

*

Archangel Gabriel.

Gabriel is often depicted with a musical instrument. This is possibly due to the fact that Gabriel is seen as a herald.

It was Gabriel who announced the forth coming birth of Jesus Christ and who channelled the Qur'an to Mohammed. (Peace be upon him)

In the Jewish teachings it is Gabriel who came to the aid of the people and parted the Red Sea to enable the Hebrews to escape from the Pharaoh.

More recently Gabriel came to awaken Joan of Arc to the needs of the Dauphin of France.

When Archangel Gabriel's energy is present s/he is often associated with the colour yellow or gold although when I have experienced his/her energy I have seen a beautiful pale fresh green.

When you connect to Gabriel notice the

colour that you can sense around him/her.

The meaning of his/her name is

GOD IS MY STRENGTH

*

*

Archangel Raphael.

Raphael is known as the Healing Archangel.

Call on Archangel Raphael when you need help with any issue concerning health, physically, emotionally, mentally or spiritually.

When Archangel Raphaels energy is present you will often see the most beautiful deep emerald green.

He has an army of healing angels.

The meaning of his name is

GOD HAS HEALED

*

*

Archangel Uriel

Uriel is very helpful with all paperwork issues.
Also with any legal issues or disputes.

He will always be fair and just in his ministrations
and only ever for your highest good.

His energy is very strong. When Archangel Uriel is
around you may see yellows and oranges.

The meaning of his name is

FIRE OF GOD

*

There are many more that I could mention but the four above tend to be the ones that are well known throughout the world.

However there is another Archangel that I will mention at this stage due to the fact that I will be mentioning her later in this book.

*

Archangel Jophiel

I work with Jophiel most of the time as her energy
brings grace and beauty to the spoken word.

Jophiel will help to find the correct words with the correct meaning so that the words do not offend but are understood and digested.

Therefore if you need to have a sensitive conversation with perhaps a tutor, partner, wife, husband, in-law, child, parent, boss etc.. then Archangel Jophiel is at hand to help.

Call on her to help you through a difficult
situations to get your point across.

*

At this moment in time we have been given extra help and guidance by God to lift our planets energy and allow in more light.

We have been sent this extra energy from the Angelic realm on a phenomenal scale, not only from this universe but from others as well. It is widely understood that the vibrational frequency of this planet needs to be lifted and to help with this quest, our creator has sent us this amazing gift of extra Angelic help.

As humans, we live in a three dimensional world. We use our three dimensional senses in every aspect of our lives our Sight, Sound, Touch, Taste and Smell.

As we have already mentioned, every physical thing that we have on this planet is made of energy and has a density and a vibrational frequency that we can use our senses to see, sense or feel. Plants, Trees, Animals, Humans, Rocks, Water and even the Air we breathe.

Each different substance vibrates at a different frequency but by using our normal senses we are only aware of the frequencies within our three dimensional range.

The Angels vibrational frequency is higher than most humans can see. But with focus and commitment we can train ourselves to be more aware of their presence. Their energy is always around us. It is full of love, peace and harmony. But due to the complexity if the modern world that we exist in, we often ignore or just don't notice their loving presence.

You will have perhaps noticed that I refer to the Archangels already mentioned as he, she or s/he, her/him. Angels will show themselves to us as either male, female or neither depending what energy we require. Therefore I have used the gender that they show themselves to me as I write about them in this book. You may see their energy differently to how they show themselves to me, different gender, different colour energy. It will be relevant to your situation or what you need to help you move forward in your life.

Angels and Archangels will change their appearance if it helps to get their message across to you.

Although the Angelic Realm reside in another dimension just outside of our own three dimensional world, we now have been given tools to use, to tap into this dimension and find out what our Angels want us to know, to connect with us on a different level, a deeper connection than we have had before.

We can also use our extra senses, the inner senses that we all have, to give us information about the people and situations around us. These are called 'Our four Clairs.'

Clairsentient – inner feeling,

Clairvoyance – inner seeing,

Clairaudience – inner hearing,

Claircognizant - inner knowing.

These extra senses are what the Angelic realm use on a regular basis to connect to us. We may call it our sixth sense or our gut reaction, our gut feeling etc.. but once you are aware that this is one of the ways our Angels get their messages across then we can start to take a bit more notice of these inner senses.

We all have these extra senses but some of us only use one or two of them, and we can all put our hands up to ignoring those inner senses at some point in our lives and possibly regretting it.

We can do a simple test to see which inner senses you use.

What is your favourite memory of your school days? (Use this space to write.)

Where is your favourite place to take a walk?

What was your favourite Christmas experience?

Now look at what you have written down and see which of the inner clairs that you have used.

Did you see it, hear it, know it, or feel it?

You may have used more than one.

Is there a pattern forming. Do you tend to use one first and then another.

Once you know which clairs you use you can start taking more notice of the subtle guidance that your Angels will be using to get you to notice.

Most people have heard of Clairvoyance, the inner seeing. This sense can become a very strong once you start to notice the information that you are getting through your third eye, or inner seeing. Like anything in life, some of you will get great results straight away, others will need to practice.

If you are using your clairaudience as your main inner sense then you may have to get accustom to your Angels bombarding you with information that you can hear. You need to be aware that sometimes the Angels speak so quickly and at such a high pitch that it is difficult for us humans to understand, it can sound like ringing in your ears, similar to tinnitus. If you think that this is happening you need to ask your Angels to slow down and speak to you in a pitch that you can hear clearly.

Once you start to connect you may have to ask them to not connect with you, for example, while you are at work or while you are driving.

We all have our own Angelic guides, no matter what our beliefs. They are there with us from the moment we enter this world and stay with us till we ascend to another dimension. Some people believe that our Guardian Angel stays with us throughout all of our lifetimes.

I am often asked what the difference is between Angelic Guides and our own Guardian Angels. I decided to tune in to my Angel in prayer to ask - and this is what I was told.

Beloved one, when God Creates a Soul it is So Perfect and Precious that he surrounds it with Protection.

This Protection is what you call your Guardian Angels.

This Protection is with you from your very first incarnation and will be with you for every single incarnation that you have.

Therefore your Guardian Angels know you better than you know yourself.

They know what lessons you have signed up for.

What lessons you have already learnt or taught and what lessons you are yet to learn or teach.

Other Angelic guides will come and go, for as long as you need their help and guidance. This guidance will be replaced as you learn and teach your lessons.

Beloved child, as one of Gods blessed children you will become more enlightened as your lessons are learned, spreading the way to the light, as you learn so you teach, thus Gods will be done.

(I have changed the words thou art, thee, thy, etc.. to you and your, so that the above is easier to read)

Because we have always had our Guardian Angels with us, we feel completely comfortable with their energy surrounding us. Their love for us is total, unconditional and all encompassing. Their energy is as feather down against our skin.

We also have Angelic energies that come and go as guides. This is when many people start to notice a change in the energies around them and start to question what they see or feel. They may be with us for a short while to help us with a specific situation or over a longer period to help us though an entire cycle of our life. But it is this **change** in energy that is often the trigger to start to question, learn and grow.

One of the many gifts God has given us is the gift of 'Free Will.' It is worth mentioning at this moment that all Angels and Archangels are bound by the law of free will, just as we are. Therefore they are not allowed to help us unless we ask.

There are a few exceptions to this. If a person is in a life threatening situation but it is not time for them to pass, the Angels may step in to save that person. However we are not privy to that information, we are not consciously aware of the lessons we have signed up for. We all have lessons to learn and lessons to teach but as soon as we are born into this world we lose all conscious memory of what they are.

We just have to trust that the situations that arise within our lives are specifically engineered to allow us to learn and grow or to teach, to allow others to grow. This is how we blossom.

When our new Angelic guides start to work with us they try to get our attention by a number of different ways. Most of us have heard of Angels dropping feathers in our path.

I have been asked to share with you such an incident. In fact my very first 'Feather Gift' experience.

We have all had times in our lives when we can't see the woods for the trees, everything seems to be crashing around us and we can't see a way forward; well my first real feather gift was given to me during one of those times.

My first Feather gift...

Many years ago I was going through a very difficult time in my life. I thought my world had come to an end, my heart had been torn open and I was in deep shock. My marriage of twenty two years had come to an abrupt end and I had moved into a tiny house with my three children with minimal income.

My health was suffering which I was ignoring, desperately trying to carry on for my children's sake, but my health got worse and then, one day, I collapsed, my youngest son had to call an ambulance for me, I was exhausted mentally, emotionally and physically, I had contracted double pneumonia.

Luckily my wonderful mother dropped everything and came to the rescue. She moved in, looked after the children, and cared for me, for five weeks. Poor Dad had to fend for himself, they must have missed each other terribly, they had never been apart for more than a few days. I was so ill I didn't even know how long she had been with me. Bless her!

Thank you so much my lovely Mummy

As I started to recover and gain my strength Mum went back home, I really missed her. Still extremely weak, just climbing the stairs was a major achievement. The children were wonderful and helped where they could; but weeks turned into months and I was losing hope of ever regaining my strength or living a normal life. I felt so alone. Then one day as I walked from the car to my front door I looked up to heaven and said

*'Angels **if** you are there I really need you to **send me a sign**.'* in my minds voice I continued, *' I need to know you are there. Please help me. I'm so tired, I can't go on like this'*

I felt so weak and my future seemed so bleak that I started to weep. As I opened the gate to the garden, slowly walking towards the front door I could see the most beautiful large pale cream feather lying in the middle of my front door step, it was about eight inches long and curled at the end with a slightly darker shade of beige at the tip. I had never seen such a beautiful feather. As I picked it up, I knew my Angels were with me. I was no longer alone. My tears of desperation turned into tears of joy and hope.

As I closed my door, clasping my gift, I felt secure, I felt safe and protected, a feeling of deep peace and calm surrounded me and I realised that this, was the first time in many years, that I had felt safe.

As I looked at my feather I couldn't work out what sort of bird it had come from, and yet, at the same time I realised that I had been given this beautiful gift, as a sign, to show me that it was definitely sent by the Angels.

If they had sent me a feather from a local bird I might have been tempted to dismiss it as a coincidence.

I now know that there are no coincidences, just messages and opportunities sent from God, via the Angels, for us to notice or act upon.

Thank you Angels for my beautiful feather.

My life now is unrecognisable to the existence I once endured. The Angels have had an enormous part in that transformation.

I now know that it was Archangel Uriel that was with me that day; he stayed with me for the next five years, along with other Archangels, Angels and guides.

I felt truly blessed

Another incident involving feather gifts was when I was driving back from an Ascended Masters workshop in Wales, with a fellow lightworker.

During the workshop Archangel Michael had been using my travelling companion to speak through, or to channel through, and, whilst in meditation, we were told that we were to take a feather from Michaels wing as a gift, and to use it to call on him whenever we needed to.

As we sat in meditation we all felt the presence of Michael and felt the feather being placed in our hands. It was an amazing experience.

My second feather gift

As we were driving along we were chattering away about the different experiences that we had at the workshop over the past few days and in particular, started to discuss Archangel Michaels presence at the workshop and to our surprise white feathers started to appear in front of us.

A third gift

One or two at first but then they came thick and fast. We couldn't believe our eyes it was just like confetti. They seemed to be coming straight down from the clouds, feather snow.

Everything seemed to be in slow motion, beautiful white feathers all around us dancing in the breeze.

Slowly it subsided and we continued on our journey with the odd one or two feathers floating past now and then.

A little while later, a few miles down the road we came to a duel carriageway, and both burst out laughing as we overtook a lorry, that was carrying a cargo of white chickens.

'*Well*' laughed my companion *'they had to get them from somewhere.*

They must have been listening to us talking about Archangel Michael and sent us the feathers as a reminder that they are always with us!

Since that journey I have followed chicken lorries a number of times, and had the odd white feather float past, but never to the extreme of that special day.

These are just a couple of examples of feather gifts that I have experienced but there are many more. I will often walk into a room and there will be a little feather in the middle of the floor or on the chair that I had been sitting on only moments before. Sometimes I will be preparing for a client or workshop and as I glance out of the window a white feather will gently float past. I always smile as I know that it is a little message for me. I am surrounded by Angels. I am surrounded by Gods love.

If you haven't had this type of experience connected to your Angels then all you have to do is ask your Angels to send you feather messages.

Beloved Angels please send this reader 'Feather Messages'
so that they may know you are with them.

Remember intention is key!!!

If your intention is pure and you ask for messages from your Angels, they will show you that you are not alone. If your intention is pure then you can learn to feel when your Angels are around, they will show you. Just remember intention is the key. Keep your intention pure. We will learn how to tune in to the Angels later in the book.

Another way that our Angels communicate with us is through touch. Have you ever felt as if someone touched your hair and you turn around to see who it was, but there is no one there?

One of my Angelic Guides is called Samuel. He is strong and tall and is usually at my left shoulder. He often speaks to me when I am working and occasionally buts in when I am channelling messages from my clients Angels.

Samuel shows me that he is there by touching my shoulder or back. Sometimes he gently pushes me out of the way if I am giving a Reiki session and he wants to work on the client as well.

He often leaves handprints or indentations on the blanket in the area he is working on. My clients will say

'I knew you were at my feet but I could also feel your hands on my head, or shoulders at the same time...'

I then explain that I am not the only one working on them and they understand.

It might have been their first experience with the Angels but they always enjoy it.

The energy of the Angels is always so full of love, as you become accustom to their energy you will come to recognise it.

©Angel of the Rose. Copyright Rev. Jodi Cross 2012

CHAPTER 2.

Grounding and Balancing, Connecting with Energy.

Before we continue, we need to learn how to ground ourselves and balance our energy. This is part of our preparation to connect to the angelic realm.

*Visualisations (*a picture or pictures in your mind's eye) are a very helpful aid as you learn to connect and ground yourself. They help you to keep your focus on the energy of the moment, rather than past issues or future possibilities. I will walk you through this in case you have not done this before.

First of all I want you to imagine that you are rooting yourself to the earth.

Close your eyes and use your minds eye to see yourself as you start this process.

Make sure you are sitting with both feet fully on the ground or on the floor.

Feel the energy of the earth as you visualise roots sprouting from your feet, gently swirling down, through the earth, to the very core of earths energy, becoming stronger and brighter as your roots approach the very centre diamond of light and energy, at the core of our mother earth, vibrating and pulsating with the very essence of life.

Once you feel that you have connected to the mother earth energy allow her energy to connect to your energy.

Feel the gentle pulsing energy, flow upwards through your physical body.

Feel the connection vibrating through you in perfect harmony with your own energy. Feeling focused, feeling grounded, feeling connected, feeling whole and complete.

Now you are grounded.

Enjoy the feeling of being connected. Get use to using this connection whenever you feel the need to ground yourself and focus on bringing yourself together.

Grounding is an excellent tool to use when you need to focus on day to day issues.

When you have become comfortable with this connection and have used it a few times. Then we can take it a step further for a full energy connection.

Only read this next section when you are in a place of relaxation. If not then skip it and come back to it when you have the time and you are in the right place.

Some people find this exercise quite emotional and it can also be time consuming.

We are all individual with individual energy needs.

This time we are going to connect with the Mother Earth energy and the Father Creator energy.

To do this you may wish to switch off the TV, radio, computer, switch off the phone etc.. so that you can completely concentrate on your energetic connection.

©Angel of the Ever Changing Waters. Copyright Rev. Jodi Cross 2012

Use this page to jot down any experiences when you try this next connection. (pages 28 – 31)

We start with connecting to the Mother Earth energy, so again you need to be sitting with both feet on the floor.

Legs and ankles, arms and hands, uncrossed.

It is important to allow the energy to flow freely, in and around, the body.

Feel the energy of the earth as you visualise roots from your feet gently swirling down, through the earth, to the very core of Mother Earths energy, becoming stronger and brighter as your roots approach the very centre diamond of light and energy, at the core of our Mother Earth. Vibrating and pulsating with the very essence of life. Feel Mother Earths' energy pulsing, gently flowing upwards through your physical body. Feel the connection vibrating through you. Now as you feel her energy pulsing through your body, visualise the energy becoming brighter so that you can see this wonderful gentle white energy as a light glowing through your very core, every cell energized. Visualise the white light reach the top of your head and see its gentle glow through your crown. As you focus on your crown of white gentle light, notice how it radiates upward, up through your higher self, getting stronger and brighter, up through your Angels and Guides, so strong, so bright, up through the Holy Spirit reaching the Father Creator energy and connecting Father and Mother energy through you.

Notice how connected you feel.

The vibrating, pulsating gentle light, so strong, so bright, running through your physical body, back and forth, from Mother Earth to Father Creator. The ebb and flow of, the essence of life, the energy of life, feeding you, nourishing and revitalising your energy, it is balancing your body as it travels back and forth through you.

This energy connection is of pure love.

Can you sense a shift in your body? Feel how alive you are, feel how connected you are, feel how focused you are, feel how balanced you have become.

Enjoy this connection of pure love.

You need now to visualise your Father and Mother energy gradually condensing. As if a caring unseen hand is gently guiding the energy down from Father and up from Mother. As the energy passes back down through your crown you can feel your crown close, strong and hard. As the energy passes back up through your feet and up through your body. Visualise and feel the energy meet as a sphere of love placed gently in your heart.

You are now filled with love and light.

Gently place your hands across your heart.

Take a few moments to readjust to your newly balanced body.

You will only gain the energy that you need, and that your body can cope with. This is because you will only be allowed to take what is for your highest good.

Not only will you feel energised you may also experience a release.

As I explained earlier this exercise can sometimes be quite emotional.

Don't worry if this happens to you, it is quite normal. See the release as a blessing. As positive.

You now need to gently release from this connection.

You can do this by expressing your gratitude, to God, for this energetic boost of his love and the balancing of your body.

©Angel of Inner Strength. Copyright Rev. Jodi Cross 2012

CHAPTER 3.

How can I contact my Guardian Angel?

First of all you must recognise that your Guardian Angel or Angels are always with you and always have been.

Therefore the energy that they emit is an energy that you feel completely at one with. This is why many people say that they can't feel their Angels presence.

If an energy has always been with you, then it is only if it disappears that you would notice the difference. And don't worry it will never disappear.

Over the years of being here on this planet, in this lifetime, there will have been times when your Angels have stepped in, to guide and protect you, without you realising it.

If you think back I'm sure you will be able to think of an instance that something has happened, that made you think that you were being looked after by an unseen helper.

So many times I hear people say - *I was so lucky * * * * * happened – or – I can't believe It, someone must be watching* *over me, guess what? * * * * * has happened– or – I shouldn't be here but by some miracle * * * * * has happened – or – Thank God I didn't do * * * * * something told me not to.*

Do any of these sound familiar? Whether or not we can think of an example, we have all had experiences with our Angels.

So now, if you feel the need to nurture and deepen your relationship with these amazing beings you need to open your mind to all possibilities.

We have already practised connecting to Mother and Father energy so now we need to learn how to feel the connection to our Guardian Angel, then recognise the feeling when connecting, so that it becomes a natural part of our daily life and your Angels will know when you are open and consciously want their help. So let us begin.

To do this we need to take ourselves off to a quiet area. Away from the TV, computer, radio, children, partners or any other disturbance.

If you have some relaxing music that you can put on quietly in the background, then do so now. Angels love gentle melodic music. It changes the energy in the room. If you have ever been to have a pamper treatment, you will no doubt remember the therapist having gentle soothing melodic music in the background to calm the energy in the room.

Go and get a pen and paper, so that you can write down anything that comes through. Write it down straight away and then you won't forget anything even if it doesn't seem to make any sense at the time. Don't worry if you can't get hold of pen and paper; try to find it for next time or use the back pages of this book.

Now find a comfortable place to sit or even lie down if you would feel more comfortable.

Make sure you don't have legs, feet or arms crossed.

If you want to start with connecting to Mother, Father, energy first then do so but it is not necessary.

Take a deep slow breath and say either out loud or in your minds voice

'Guardian Angel please allow me to feel your presence now'

Take another deep slow breath and allow yourself to relax and gently drift with the music. Don't try to force anything, just relax.

Close your eyes. Then visualise your Guardian Angel standing behind you. As you picture this in your mind's eye, visualise the Angelic wings gently wrapping around you.

As you relax you may feel warmth, or coolness, surround you, you may be aware of a temperature change in the room. If you drift into a deeper relaxation or sleep, you may see colours or little sparkles of light. Some people even feel something brush their cheek or arm. Don't be alarmed, don't forget you asked for some form of presence to be felt.

Intention is everything so if you are not in the right frame of mind or the Angels feel that this is not the best time for you to experience their energy then you may have to wait for them to show you at another time.

The important thing is that they know that you want to build and strengthen your relationship with them and feel their energy on a more physical level.

Like anything we try for the first time, some people get great results first time others have to wait and practice. This is why keeping a journal of your experiences is helpful.

Remember the Angels will only give you messages for your highest good, they are always full of positive energy.

If you would like to know what your Angel or Angels are called then once you can feel the energy around you, ask in your minds voice.

'What name shall I use when I want to connect to you.'

If the Angelic name is too high a pitch for you to hear or understand, then they will give you a name, or word that pops into your head, that they want you to use for connecting to them. Often it is a name that is not connected to any of your friends or family members. That way they know that when you are trying to connect with them, you will use the word or name that they have given to you.

Enjoy this connection. Enjoy the love and compassion that you will feel as you connect.

Remember intention is everything. If your intention is pure, then your connection is pure.

Write down everything that happens and see how it changes over a few months.

When you ask for a name and you are given a name that you perhaps feel is not an angelic name, please don't pre judge.

The reason I say this to you is that over the years I have heard many people exclaim

When I asked

'What name shall I use when I want to connect to you.'

they said ' . . . . . . ' surely this can't be right'

I will give you an example of such a story.

A very experienced lightworker with over forty years experience shared that when she was learning to connect to the Angelic Realm she asked what name she could use to connect and she was given the words 'FENCE POST'. She decided that she must be doing something wrong and tried again. She still got the same words.

She was getting impatient; she wanted a graceful feminine angelic name. 'FENCE POST' did not fit the bill, 'FENCE POST' in her opinion, was not a suitable name for an angel.

Then the voice that gave her the words showed himself to her. He was a huge Afro/Caribbean man about eight feet tall with huge feet. She especially noticed his huge feet.

This was not at all what she had expected. As he showed himself to her he gave her a huge smile. Everything about him was huge. What a shock!

However over the years she has come to expect the unexpected and learned a very strong lesson in pre judgements.

It is very important to learn the lesson about pre judgements as you may also experience things that you have already made different judgements about and therefore feel that something is wrong when actually all that was wrong was your own judgement.

Remember not all angels have wings.

God sends us angels in all shapes and forms.

We all have our own expectations as to what our own Guardian Angels will look like and sound like but please remember the story above just in case God has other ideas.

Do you know the saying –

We make a decision and God laughs !

or

How to make God laugh - tell him your plans!

We don't remember why we are here this time round. We have no conscious memory of what lessons we need to learn in this lifetime; we have no conscious memory of what we need to teach in this lifetime.

We all have lessons to learn and lessons to teach but no conscious memory of either so **now** that we know that, we can see why it is **so** important to have an open mind about how our lives should pan out.

Be flexible. God Knows Everything.

Trust and allow yourself to be guided by Him and his messengers.

Remember anything that comes from God is filled with love and light and is always for your highest good.

One way the Angelic Realm speaks to us is through dreams and repartition. You may have a dream about something that seems random, then see something related, hear words on the radio that are related and so on. This is their way of getting you to notice. Pointing you in the right direction.

Remember your Angels love you unconditionally, no matter what.

Their messages will always come from love, peace and harmony. This is important for you to remember as you start to notice the signs that they send you.

If you start to link in to them on a regular basis you will gradually become more aware of their presence in all that you do.

©Angel of the Light. Copyright Rev. Jodi Cross 2012

Chapter 4

What is Ego?

One question that comes up at Angel workshops is

'How do I know if it is my Angels that are sending me messages and not something else?'

Angels will never send you any message that is not for your highest good. If you are getting negative mind chatter then you are talking to ego.

Ok. At this point we need to understand ego.

Ego is that little inner voice that we all have that feeds on negative thoughts, negative words and negative deeds. It is the little voice of fear, guilt, doubt and inner turmoil. We all have it, but the important thing is not to feed it.

It feeds on our fear, guilt, shame, lack of self worth, lack of self esteem and so on. It tells us we are not good enough, we can't do it, etc..

So many of us feed our ego without even realising it, with self sabotage and negative mind chatter, we allow these unhelpful thoughts to go round and around in our minds voice, so that we start believing our own inner voice of doubt.

How many of us have bought into this self sabotage, this negative way of thinking. Have you heard yourself say

' I can't do that. I'm not good enough. I'm not clever enough.' 'I'm not fat enough' I'm not thin enough' 'She won't like me' 'He won't like me' etc.. etc..

This in turn can cause all sorts of repercussions. We start to feel sad, we start to feel tired, we hold tension in our bodies as we go round and round on the negative merry-go-round.

We are talking ourselves out of enjoying this wonderful life.

Our negative mind chatter can affect every decision we make, it becomes a habit. We are so good at putting ourselves down.

It's time to stop!

Think about how you use negative mind chatter against yourself.

You are probably unaware of the effect this has on you. You are probably unaware that you even do think about yourself in a negative way.

Think about the people around you; Your friends or perhaps your family. Who is it that is always saying.

I can't do that.

I'm no good at that sort of thing.

Things always go wrong for me.

Are you in a position where a loved one is always putting you down. Often this can happen without the person realising the damage that is done by a few throwaway remarks.

How can we stop this habit?

Well the Angels can help, or should I say the Angels and Archangels.

This is a wonderful tool for you to use in many different situations. Take a deep breath and centre yourself. Then ask

Archangel Michael and Archangel Jophiel, please be with me here in this moment to protect me from ego and all negativity that is not for my highest good.

Initially if it helps you to visualise them standing beside you or behind you then do so.

Visualisation is a very powerful tool to use to help you get started and your Angels will be aware of what you are trying to achieve. Just remember intention is key.

This is not a game these Archangels are incredibly powerful.

There are different ways to ask for protection. We have discussed the way to protect yourself from ego. But there are other ways in which these Archangels can help.

You can ask Archangel Michael and Archangel Jophiel to protect you in lots of different situations, for example if you know that you are going to have to speak to someone, and the conversation may be difficult then ask for protection.

You may need to speak to an aggressive neighbour, your mother in law, your difficult to reach teenager, your stressed boss, your frustrated toddler, your tired partner, your un co-operative bank manager.

Whatever the situation, if you feel in any way concerned or nervous, ask for help, ask for protection.

The reason that I suggest that you ask both Archangels for help with these particular situations, is that Michael brings the strength that you need and Jophiel brings in the beauty and grace to soften the situation.

Another popular way of protecting yourself is to ask the Angels or Archangels, to wrap you in a bubble of love.

Use your mind's eye if it helps you to hold the image that you are wrapped in a bubble.

A variation on the above is to ask to be wrapped in a protective cloak with a hood to completely cover you that only love can get through. It's important to ask that love can still get through as you don't ever want to stop love from getting through to you.

My preferred choice of protection is to ask the Angels to weave a protective mist around, above and below me that only love can get through. I visualise a pink mist completely protecting me as I work.

As well as asking for protection, don't forget to also ask your angels to guide your speech when you have to have that difficult conversation.

This prayer to the Angels is very powerful and creates incredible results.

'Dear Angels Please help me to speak my truth and help me to find the words that will get my message across and be understood, but that will not hurt or distress.'

'Thank you for always being there for me.

Thank you, Thank you, Thank you.'

It is important to remember, that although the Angels are always with us, they can only help us with specific situations if we **ask** for their help.

Don't forget that one of the greatest gifts God has given us is 'Free Will.' Don't assume that just because the Angels know your intention or situation that they will step in and help. It doesn't work like that.

You have to **ask**, and you have to be **specific**.

For example, I'm sure you have heard about the parking Angels. If you get into your car and start driving to the shopping centre asking

'Please Angels can I have a parking space'?

You will probably find that, as you are driving along, a space appears just at the side of the road as you pass it.

You didn't specify where or when you needed the parking space. Don't forget that the Angelic realm do not have time and space constraints in the same way that we do. You must be specific when you ask.

The Angels are wonderful helpers and don't forget to ask for their help if you need them at work.

My husband often asks for their help when he is working. If he has a difficult day, or a particular problem that he has come up against. He will call on their help.

He said that he felt awkward at first, even slightly embarrassed at asking the Angels for help, but he has been so amazed at their response he talks to his Angels and often asks for their help now.

Having explained to you that you can call on your Angels for all sorts of things, there are a couple of things to keep in mind.

First of all, the Angels will only help us if it is for our highest good. Remember intention is key.

Sometimes we have to go through situations to learn important lessons and grow.

Sometimes these lessons can seem hard and painful, but long term we will benefit from having experienced them.

The second thing to remember is gratitude. Gratitude has a high vibrational frequency. Angels resonate with the vibration of gratitude. Always thank them for their help and support. It is so important; I can't stress this point enough. Please don't forget to thank them, and more importantly mean it.

*'Beloved Angels thank you for being with me today and helping me with * * * * * '*

'Thank you Angels for your help and support,

I really appreciate it'

Thank you, Thank you, Thank you.

When I am teaching at workshops, students sometimes say that they feel uncomfortable asking for an Archangel to help them. They feel that their particular problem is perhaps not as important as somebody else's therefore they don't want to take up an Archangels time away from more important issues.

Please don't worry. You must remember that we live in a different dimension to the Angelic Realm.

In our Realm we have something called TIME. We live our lives by it. We work by it. We set ourselves goals against it. We have also set ourselves parameters around SPACE. We have set rules about space. The space we live in. Our personal space, our comfort zone.

Our society has programmed its self to such a degree that it has a very narrow expectation of time and space. Time and Space are things we have created to set ourselves boundaries. These are our rules, in our world, in our dimension. We are the only species on this planet that live our lives by clock watching. What time we eat, what time we sleep, what time we work and so on.

We are in a very exciting space and time cycle at the moment, for at last Quantum Physics is shortening the gap between three dimensional reality and quantum reality.

The Angelic Realm are not confined by 'Time or Space' they are able to be in multiple places at any given moment in time. A million different people could call on a particular Archangel at any time, in any location across our globe, and that particular Archangel will be there with each of those million people simultaneously.

This will not in any way detract from any other individuals needs or help. By asking an Archangel to use their power to help you, it does not mean that their power and energy is being used up by you and that someone around the other side of the world will only get a reduced energy.

How incredible! Aren't we blest to have such an amazing amount of love based energy that can be with us in the blink of an eye.

At the beginning of this chapter I asked you to open your mind to all possibilities. This is an area that needs for you to be more open minded.

It is understandable that we should think the way we do because of the limitations we have made within our own structured lives, society and world.

You will be amazed at the way your Angels can help you navigate your way through life.

Your world, as you see it, will change dramatically as you start to work with your Angels and leave any negativity habits behind.

CHAPTER 5

Recognising and working with different Energies

When you first call on an Archangel you will probably notice a change in the energy around you. Do you remember when we were talking about our own Guardian Angels energy, how we are so use to it being around us that we don't even notice it.

As you start to work with the Archangels you will notice each one has a slightly different feel, or energy.

In your mind's eye you may see colours. Some people see very clear definitions of colour. Others see translucent suggestions of colour. Often the colour will become stronger as you ask for the Angel or Archangel to help you or work with you.

Don't worry if you don't see colours straight away. We all have different ways we connect and at different levels.

Feeling an Angels presence is a wonderful experience. You may feel a change in temperature, a sudden breath of cool air or a feeling of warmth, or just have a knowing that there is a presence in the room as you meditate with them. Their energy is always full of love.

You can practice connecting to the different Angels by first connecting to your Guardian Angel in the way we discussed earlier, and then asking a specific Archangel to connect to you.

It is important at this stage that you only work with one Archangel at a time. This allows you to really get to know the energy of each individual Archangel.

Please don't move on to another Archangel until you feel completely comfortable with the energy. When you start to connect to an Archangel, please behave in a respectful manner. Let your own Guardian Angel know what it is that you are trying to achieve.

Having already connected to your own Guardian Angel take a deep slow breath and enjoy the energetic embrace, then take another deep slow breath and say.

*Beloved Guardian Angel, I would like
to connect to the energy*

of Archangel .... so that I recognise and experience

his / her energy.

Use *visualisation (*a picture in your mind's eye) to see the Archangel come forward, and ask for their angelic energy to merge with your energy. Notice any change's. You may be given a colour or feeling that is different to your own Guardian Angel's energy.

Explore the differences. Use all of your senses.

Keep a pad of paper and pen handy in case you are given a message.

> *Beloved Archangel .... do you*
> *have a message for me.*

You may be given a message or just a knowing of the love that is radiating from the amazing being of Light that God has sent to connect to you.

Once you have connected to a specific Archangel a few times and you feel that you fully understand their presence and energy. Then you can repeat the process with another Archangel.

As you have only just started to connect at this level, it is best to start connecting with the five Archangels already mentioned.

After you have connected. It is important to remember to sign off or log out, so that you are not leaving yourself open to allowing other energies to connect with you.

Remember the importance of gratitude.

> *Blessed Archangel .... I can feel your*
> *love and light. Thank you for allowing me*
> *to connect to your energy today.*
>
> *Thank you, Thank you, Thank you.*

Then, when you have finished, in your mind's eye see your energy centres close. Use visualisation to close the link. If you feel drawn to physically cut through the energetic cord use your hand in a sword like manner to disconnect your energy from your angel or archangel, in a sweeping motion. It is important to close your connection so that you are not open to other energies that you have not invited to connect to you.

After a while, when you have learned about the differences of the Archangels energies and are able to identify each one, you may find that you connect to other energy. Ascended Masters often come through on a similar frequency to the Angelic frequency.

Today, as I continue to write this book, I have been joined by Mother Mary and Archangel Gabriel's energy. Such a Blessing.

'Thank you Blessed Mother Mary and Archangel Gabriel for connecting with my energy today.'

Many years ago, when I was in deep relaxation, meditating, Mother Mary came forward and placed a beautiful Pink Rose, a fully opened bloom, in the palm of my hand, it filled my hand and fingers, and was the most beautiful 'pale' pink, and yet the colour seemed so rich, so full.

As I looked at the gift I had been given, it filled my outstretched hand completely. It also filled my heart. So perfect and beautiful, so soft and yet the energy within it felt enormous, felt strong, felt deep. So strong and yet so delicate and fragile. I was concerned that I might damage it but as soon as I had that thought, the rose gently melted into my hand becoming part of me. Now whenever Mother Mary comes to me, I open my hand to show her the rose and she smiles.

Another gift that I was given from an Ascended Master was from Ascended Master Hilarion. Again I was in deep meditation and he stepped forward and placed something around my neck. I couldn't see what it was, I just knew that it was radiating gold light and energy. Each time Master Hilarion visited me either in meditation or while I slept, I would raise my head and his gift at my throat would fill the air with the radiance and energy of gold light. I asked him what my gift was or what it signified but he would just smile.

After a while I stopped asking as I realised that it was not for me to know; but then one day he came to me and as I lifted my head the energy around us both changed and the gold light became a vortex, becoming stronger and stronger until both of our energies were transmuted to become the gold energy of the vortex.

It seemed to change into a double helix of energy and we both were completely dissolved into the double helix of gold light, the DNA of infinity, the very strands of life.

After a while we returned to our three dimensional state and I realised that whatever the gift had been, it's energy was now part of me.

The reason I have shared this story with you is so that if you are given a gift from the Angels or an Ascended Master you will not be afraid and can accept it with love and grace. You will only be given gifts for your highest good.

All gifts from the Angelic realm or the Ascended Masters are for your highest good and are filled with love. God uses both Angels and Ascended Masters to help guide you, always from a place of love.

Some gifts are huge while others are just little reminders so that you know that you are not alone, but both sorts of gifts are equally filled with love.

CHAPTER 6

Healing with the Angels

When you connect to your Angelic guides you can ask for healing for a specific issue or problem. The reason I say issue or problem is that you may think you have a problem in one area of your life or physical being but the Angels can see the root of the problem and will always start healing from the heart which is not necessarily what you have asked for.

Remember - They will always heal from the heart not from the lips.

When people come to me for an Angel Reading or Angel Therapies session I explain to them that it may be quite an emotional experience for them.

The Angels will work with me, using me as a channel to unblock anything that is stopping them from moving on.

The Angels guide people to me who need the help I can give, just as the Angels will guide people to you to help you be either healed or to heal, or as often happens, both. Angelic healing takes place on many different levels, past, present and future.

I have met many Lightworkers on my journey through life, some I have worked with, some I have learned from, some I have taught, but I am always amazed at the diversity of people who are drawn to work with the Angels.

Although you may have bought this book just to learn a little about the Angelic realm and how to connect, after reading it and digesting the content you may find that you are able to offer advice and help to your family and friends to enhance and strengthen their connection with their Angels, whatever your situation, wherever you work, wherever you live, you will meet people who may benefit from the knowledge you now have. You may decide to buy a copy of this book for them, or suggest they read your copy.

The Angels have asked me to get this out to as many people as possible so please share with your friends. This book is a starting point for you to become more enlightened, trusting in your own judgments and connecting with God through his essence, his energy, his Angelic Army of messengers, his beloved Angels.

Never forget you are a perfect child of God and his love for you is total. We have all been created, We are all one, we are all connected.

If you have practiced and consciously connected to the Archangels, as I have suggested earlier in the book, then you will already be aware of Archangel Raphael's healing energy. He may have already worked with you, to start your healing.

Archangel Raphael has an army of Healing Angels that are available for you to work with whenever you feel the need.

We have already discussed ego and the damage it can do if it is fed and allowed to grow.

Remember - Intention is everything.

Do not allow negative mind chatter to block any healing that you need. Keep your thoughts, words and deeds controlled. Make sure they are in Positive mode.

Each and every day of your life your thoughts, words and deeds must always stay positive. This is an important part of your healing.

As the Angels are dictating this book, they are most insistent that you take ownership of your state of health. This is for your highest good. You might find this a chore to start with but, if you can train yourself to do this, you will reap the benefits. Your mood will lighten; your enjoyment of life will increase. When you consciously stay in a positive mind set, you relax your hold on past struggles.

The things from the past that make you sad or angry have a better chance of staying in the past if you release the emotion that is attached to the event, or person.

This is all part of your healing.

If you do not release all the sorrow from your past it will just keep coming up and reminding you, again and again. Sapping your energy, taking away the joy that your life should be filled with, sometimes this can be so subtle that you are not even aware that it is still affecting you and you wonder why things keep coming around, again and again.

It's time to get off the emotional roundabout.

Every action requires a reaction. If you are **always** reacting to something or someone in the **same** way, then the end result will **always** be the **same**.

Therefore you need to take away the reaction and **change** it. By doing this you automatically **change** the outcome.

Again this may be difficult to remember at first but with practice you will find that it becomes second nature and things will be different for you.

Let's put this into practice – for example

Your work colleague is always moaning about - the boss - his wife - his kids. He makes a bee line for your desk every morning and moans. You have to sit there and listen. By the time he leaves you are feeling heavy with all that he has dumped on you. As the day progresses you notice some of the things he had mentioned and you feel even heavier. The energy in the entire office is negative; you feel sorry for him but don't see how you can help and you try to avoid him as much as possible.

So how can you change this situation into 'positive mode'?

- First of all you need to make sure that you are not taking ownership of his problems.

They are his problems not yours, it is his anger, not yours, it is his frustration, not yours, it is his ego, not yours. You have to let it waft over you. Ignore the emotion that he uses as he is speaking in this way.

His issues and problems are **his** to take all the responsibility for; you must not take any responsibility for his problems.

Once you realise that you do not have to take any ownership or responsibility of his issues, he no longer has the ability to interfere with your feelings, your mood, your energy.

You are in charge of how you feel. Use your inner strength. Ask for divine protection, as we have already discussed. Stay in the positive mode of being.

If you are still not able to space yourself from this bombarding of negative energy then it might help you to imagine him dressed as a clown, with Micky Mouse ears and pink fizzy hair.

This work colleague example above, is of a type of behaviour that you may be able to relate to, you may have a particular person that you can think of who behaves in a similar way, therefore you can use the same suggestions to deal with the negativity.

You just need to remember a few things to help you stay in the positive mode. Use the visualisation above and see how you feel the next time a similar thing happens to you, and remember that you do not take ownership or responsibility of his/her problems.

- Next ask yourself why?

Why does he/she behave like that? Is he/she at breaking point and just needs a friendly ear to hear about his/her troubles? Is he/she lonely and you are the only person in the work place that listens to him/her? Has he/she been bought up in a house of negative people and he/she doesn't know any other way to behave? Does he/she have a *real* problem with his/her boss or is being negative about him just his/her way of protecting himself/herself?

People often go into attack mode when they feel threatened. By suggesting that others are lacking in some way it makes them feel stronger. I'm sure at some point in your life you have experienced a situation where someone's behaviour has been attack in order to defend. However this is exactly how ego controls. That little voice of doubt, that little voice of fear, that little voice of rejection will feed its self and grow stronger if it is not stopped. As we have already discussed ego is extremely destructive if it is not checked and stopped.

There may have been times in your life, after you have perhaps experienced some form of trauma and without realising it, you perhaps have fallen into the ego trap. You start reliving the trauma and make excuses for not going forward with your life.

Ego will use your sadness to feed and grow using all the negative emotions against you.

Once you understand this, you can stop it from controlling your life!

If you have experienced a time when ego controlled your life, then you will be able to see it in others and therefore help them to come out of the dark, back to the light.

This is not a simple task and for some people it can take many months even years to start believing in themselves, trusting and feeling confident in themselves again.

The reasons that the Angels have guided me to again mention ego is because of the 'real' damage that negativity has on the physical body.

When you are not at ease, then you are at Dis-ease.

When you are in a Dis-ease mode you are not functioning at your maximum capacity and are putting blocks in the way of the natural flow of your vibrational frequency. If you think of all the issues that you are holding on to, past relationships, past disappointments, past judgements, all of these issues and more are often then converted to the mind conversations that you have had, and are perhaps still having.

Many healing issues start with your own conception of who you are.

Remember you are a perfect child of God.

You are a perfect child of God. Repeat it to yourself.

'I am a perfect child of God.'

If you continue to feed yourself with self sabotaging thoughts, negative mind chatter, negative speech, negative actions, then you will stay in the state of Dis-ease.

The answer is simple. Choose to Change!

Change the way you see yourself within the world you live in. Remember you are in charge of your life. Why would you choose to live in Dis-ease. Choose to change. Choose to enjoy your life. Choose to be happy. Choose to be at peace in your heart. Choose to be at ease.

The only constant in life that God has given us is Change, and yet Change is the one thing that most of us are worried about.

Take time to really digest the sentence above - The only constant in life that God has given us is Change, and yet Change is the one thing that most of us are worried about.

Ask yourself are you one of those people who hate change?

I know I was. I now see change as a way forward to add to my life experiences. To gain a better understanding of who I am and how I can be of service to God, to my family, to the world that we call home.

Are you ready to except change?

If your answer is yes then start your new life today and relish the changes that you can make to enhance your life. You are now able to consciously connect to your Angels and Archangels, to Ascended Masters and to work on that connection for your new experiences filled with the love and light of God.

All you have to do is Trust.

All you have to do is Change.

All you have to do is see the world through the eyes of a Child filled with wonder.

Remember, you are 'A Perfect Child of God'.

Your Angels will gently guide you to a more healthful being. Allowing you to adapt at your own pace to a new way of being. Creating a new healthful energy for you to live your life in. New energy for your Mind, Body and Soul to enjoy as you blossom and grow, in the love and light of our father creator.

Part of your daily healing will be enhanced by this connection each night before you sleep.

Evening Healing Meditation.

As you prepare yourself for sleeping and you take off your outer garments, stripping away the energy of the day. Allow your mind to release all of the whole days clutter. With each garment, peel away the mental connection to your work, release it now.... , peel away the mental connection to your home, release it now.... , peel away the mental connection to your family, release it now... so that all that is left is you.

As you wash away the dust of the day, from your face, hands and body, see yourself as being cleansed from all the struggles and strains, tension and worry of the day.

As you clean your teeth and wash your mouth, feel the release of all that has been said - exchanged for a cleansed refreshing taste.

As you gently lay your body down upon your bed, lay on your back, fully stretched out. Do not cross your arms or legs as you want your energy to flow. Once you are in a comfortable position take a slow deep breath. As you exhale allow yourself to release any tension or stress of the day.

Breathe slowly in and slowly out.

Now I want you to visualise that your Angels are standing all around you, creating a circle of light, a circle of love completely surrounding you.

Now in your minds voice I want you to ask your Angels to cleanse your energy as you take another deep slow breath and release all toxins and tension that is not for your highest good.

At this point if you have a physical problem or are in pain in your physical body, as you take another breath, in your minds voice ask Archangel Raphael to be with you here in this moment to bring his Army of Healing Angels to start the healing process to (whatever part of your body that you feel needs healing) if it is for your highest good. In your mind's eye, see the Healing Angels arrive as they start to change the energy around you and within you to healing energy.

Focus your intention to each area that you feel needs healing. Feel how gentle the energy is emanating from this beautiful healing session. Allow yourself to drift off to sleep surrounded by the love and light of your Angels, Archangel Raphael and the Healing Angels for they will be working on you while you sleep for however long is necessary.

Allowing yourself to be healed in this way is a wonderful experience. Do this every night for as long as feels necessary. There is no wrong or right length of time to do this. We are all slightly different, we are unique so timing will differ from person to person.

The reason why it is important to always ask if it is for your highest good is that we have no conscious memory of what we have signed up for, this time round, so we must respect the rule and hopefully learn the lesson first time round.

As I have been writing this book or should I say scribing it for the Angels, I have been surprised at this chapter. I have questioned why the title and content? Why the emphasis on the DIY approach? And have been told that it is important that you the reader realise the strength of you own thoughts, words and deeds, and that you take some of the ownership for your own healing.

By taking responsibility for your own health, with a little guidance and energy from the Angelic realm you will also regain any power that you may have lost to ego. Self esteem, self worth, self confidence will all grow as you use the tools they have given you to use, as and when, you need them.

Start living your life in the Present.

See the beauty in all things.

Allow your past hurt or mistrust to drift away as you start your life afresh. You are not alone. You are loved beyond belief. You are strengthened by your new energy.

You are a Perfect Child of God!!!!

Be healed.

Be loved.

Be you.

Be as one.

As I come to the end of this channelling, I am reminded of something a fellow lightworker once said to me.

'My wish is that you are in, and of, love, for the rest of your lifetime here.'

At first I didn't understand what he meant. What does it mean – in and of love?

I'm sure we can all relate to being in and of love at some point in our lives, but to live your life completely in love, to live your life completely filled with the energy of love, is to be complete, is to be as one.

We are all connected, we are all created from the love of our own beloved Creator.

He has given our souls this amazing experience of living within a human form to learn our lessons, to experience his love from a different perspective, to blossom and grow to a new level of understanding.

Forever changing, forever evolving and yet forever connected.

He has created us to be unique and yet we are all one!

We may have different coloured skin, we may have different coloured eyes, we may have different coloured hair, we may choose to connect to him by saying different words, we may prefer to use different places of worship with different services and different names or signs above the doors, we may choose to use the word God or Allah or Jehovah, but we are all one, as we all come from the essence of God.

We are all Perfect Children of God.

If he wanted us to all have the same experiences, we would have been created to be all the same.

So please remember all of your brothers and sisters of this world when you ask for healing. We are all connected and always shall be whether in this dimension or another.

Therefore dear reader my wish for you is that you are

In and Of Love - Forever.

May the connection you have now, grow in strength and depth, as you continue your journey back to God, guided by his Beloved Angels. And so it is...

(A last word about the book from my Angels.)

Beloved One

We have given you this task so that your teachings may be experienced by many Earth Souls around the planet.

We have asked you to include some of your experiences so that the Earth Souls may realise that they two can experience the depth of connection that you achieve and are not afraid to do so.

We have asked you to speak of some difficult times so again your fellow Earth Souls are aware that the difficult lessons once learned can lift your energy to new heights for your growth and enlightenment.

Your light shines brightly as you fulfil this mission. Your energy will enable others to find their way back to God. May the everlasting light be with you always as you walk this road with us.

You have been told to 'Bring the People Back to My Love' this is part of your mission.

You are truly Blessed.

NOTES

NOTES

NOTES